Sara Schlenkrich

The Act on the Reform of the Market for Medicinal Products (AMNOG)

A question of power?!

Anchor Academic
Publishing

Schlenkrich, Sara: The Act on the Reform of the Market for Medicinal Products (AMNOG): A question of power?! Hamburg, Anchor Academic Publishing 2015

Buch-ISBN: 978-3-95489-359-1
PDF-eBook-ISBN: 978-3-95489-859-6
Druck/Herstellung: Anchor Academic Publishing, Hamburg, 2015

Bibliografische Information der Deutschen Nationalbibliothek:
Die Deutsche Nationalbibliothek verzeichnet diese Publikation in der Deutschen Nationalbibliografie; detaillierte bibliografische Daten sind im Internet über http://dnb.d-nb.de abrufbar.

Bibliographical Information of the German National Library:
The German National Library lists this publication in the German National Bibliography. Detailed bibliographic data can be found at: http://dnb.d-nb.de

© Anchor Academic Publishing, Imprint der Diplomica Verlag GmbH
Hermannstal 119k, 22119 Hamburg
http://www.diplomica-verlag.de, Hamburg 2015
Printed in Germany

Abstract

The Act on the Reform of the Market for Medicinal Products, which entered into force on the 1st of January 2011, brought about a fundamental change in the balance of power on the pharmaceutical market. This study therefore sets out to answer the following question: What impact does the early benefit assessment in the context of the Act on the Reform of the Market for Medicinal Products have on the stakeholders of the healthcare system?

To answer this question, this survey first presents the theoretical foundations of the law, of the early benefit assessment and the bodies involved. It then takes stock of the decisions taken to date before describing the impact on the selected stakeholders.

The following findings were reached: As the representative of the statutory health insurance funds, the Central Federal Association of Statutory Health Insurance Funds has gained in power and now decides, as a member of the Federal Joint Committee, on the added benefit of a drug and, depending on this decision, also on the future reimbursement rate. Pharmaceutical companies, however, are losing clout and must comply with the guidelines and assessments of the early benefit assessment. Patients stand to gain and lose out from the early benefit assessment. They are the ones who are ultimately dependent on the medicinal product and its improvement and benefit from a proven benefit. However, they have no say in the early benefit assessment procedure.

Contents

List of abbreviations

ACHSE	Allianz Chronischer Seltener Erkrankungen e.V. (Alliance of Chronic Rare Diseases e.V.)
AMNOG	Arzneimittelmarktneuordnungsgesetz (Act on the Reform of the Market for Medicinal Products)
AM-NutzenV	Arzneimittel-Nutzenbewertungsverordnung (Ordinance on the Early Benefit Assessment of Pharmaceuticals)
BMG	Bundesministerium für Gesundheit (Federal Ministry of Health)
BPI	Bundesverband der Pharmazeutischen Industrie e.V. (German Pharmaceutical Industry Association)
G-BA	Gemeinsamer Bundesauschuss (Federal Joint Committee)
GBE	Gesundheitsberichtserstattung des Bundes (Advisory Council on the Assessment of Developments in the Healthcare System)
GKV	Gesetzliche Krankenversicherung (Statutory Health Insurance)
HTA	Health Technology Assessment
IQWiG	Institut für Qualität und Wirtschaftlichkeit im Gesundheitswesen (Institute for Quality and Efficiency in Healthcare)
vfa	Verband Forschender Arzneimittelhersteller e.V. (German Association of Research-based Pharmaceutical Companies)

"In a healthcare distribution system with a capped budget, at the end of the day it always comes down to a question of power."

- Bernd Wegener, Chairman of the Board of the
German Pharmaceutical Industry Association (BPI)

1. Introduction

The German healthcare system is underpinned by the principle of solidarity. A health insurance fund, financed by contributions from employers[1] and employees, forms the financial basis of the system. This fund is used to pay all diagnostic and therapeutic benefits for citizens insured under statutory insurance schemes (Busse, et al., 2013, p 114). Healthcare resources are therefore limited. The financing of the fund faces a number of challenges: an increasingly aging population with increased morbidity, a decreasing number of young contributors and increased costs due to actual or supposed pharmaceutical innovations.

It is only natural therefore that the health insurance funds should be interested in scientifically proven treatments. The Federal Joint Committee (G-BA), a centralised body, decides on the eligibility of treatments for reimbursement. In order to reach a decision on the benefits of treatments that is as scientifically substantiated as possible, the G-BA commissions so-called Health Technology Assessments (HTA). HTAs are benefit assessments entailing the evaluation of existing studies and medical publications. The Institute for Quality and Efficiency in Healthcare (IQWiG) is one of the bodies entrusted with such HTAs in Germany.

In the past, high costs have been incurred in particular by the market launch of new medicinal products. To date, it was not necessary to demonstrate an additional therapeutic benefit. This changed with the Act on the Reform of the Market for Medicinal Products (AMNOG), which entered into force on the 1st of January 2011. This Act regulates the pricing of newly authorised medicinal products and thus their eligibility for reimbursement by statutory health insurance (GKV). In future, the manufacturer must demonstrate proof of an added benefit over a comparator therapy for all new medicinal products. The G-BA thus decides on the extent of the added benefit. It is assisted in its decision-making by an IQWiG benefit assessment.

---

[1] To make this survey easier to read, the generic masculine is used even when referring to both genders.

1.1 Scope

The early benefit assessment in the context of AMNOG has consequences for all stakeholders within the healthcare system. Two and a half years after its entry into force, the impact of the Act is becoming more apparent, now allowing a more discriminating analysis. This survey starts out by examining the theoretical foundations of the law and the bodies involved. This is followed by a critical analysis of the early benefit assessment of pharmaceuticals from the perspective of the health insurance funds, the pharmaceutical industry and the patients.

1.2 The central research question

What impact does the early benefit assessment in the context of AMNOG have on the stakeholders of the healthcare system in the light of the available data?

1.3 Methodology

The first part of the book will set out the theoretical background. For this purpose, the necessity of adopting the Act and its objectives will be elucidated. One aspect of the Act is the early benefit assessment, which will be explained in greater detail below. To ease understanding, the two bodies involved - the G-BA and the IQWiG – will first be presented and the structure and content of the dossier underlying an early benefit assessment clarified.

The second part of the survey will go through the available data relating to the practical experience garnered to date. It will begin with an analysis of benefit assessments already concluded, which will provide a deeper insight into the frequencies and differences observed in the granting of added benefits, illustrated by diagrams accompanied by comments. The views of three stakeholders in the assessment procedure are subsequently set out. These are: pharmaceutical companies as manufacturers of the medicinal products subject to the assessment, the health insurance funds as administrators of the finances of the healthcare system and the patients[2] who rely on pharmaceutical innovations. This should make it possible to consider the early benefit assessment from the most important angles.

---

[2] In the context of this survey, "patients" shall be defined as all insured persons who currently receive healthcare benefits.

Due to the timeliness of the topic, the limited national relevance and the relatively short period since the entry into force of the law, the literature on early benefit assessment is few and far between. The survey has therefore drawn on statements, annual reports, scientific articles, reports, etc. The author also personally participated in public hearings of the G-BA and cooperated in a workshop on "Economics and Health Technology Assessments in the area of haemophilia".

Finally, the impact of the early benefit assessment is interpreted and conclusions drawn.

2. The Act on the Reform of the Market for Medicinal Products

The steady progress in pharmaceutical treatments as a result of constantly new and, above all, costly drugs and treatment options presents a challenge for healthcare resources. That is why the health insurance funds are always on the lookout for ways of cutting their costs and, over the years, a variety of healthcare policy measures have been introduced to achieve such savings. The Act on the Reform of the Market for Medicinal Products (AMNOG), anchored in paragraph 35a of Volume 5 of the German Social Code, adopted by the German parliament on the 11th of November 2010 and in force since the 1st of January 2011, is an important instrument in this case in point.

2.1 The background of the Act

In 2009, more than 30 billion euros were spent on medicinal products, including the co-payments of the insured (Federal Ministry of Health, 2013a). A significant share of this total was incurred by innovative but also cost-intensive special preparations. "They already account for around 26 per cent of SHI's volume of medicinal products, although their share of prescription accounts for only 2.5 per cent" (German Parliament, 2010). The increase in the cost of medicinal products without a reference price is particularly high in this respect. According to Jens Baas, Chairman of the Board of the Techniker Krankenkasse health insurance fund:

> "The expenditure for this is the second largest item for the SHI. Properly applied, a good pharmaceutical therapy can be one of the most effective medical acts. The pharmaceutical industry is often seen as an innovative industry. And also in the political debate, "pharmaceuticals" are a topic that comes back time and time again. It is therefore worthwhile to continuously and carefully monitor the supply of pharmaceuticals." (Windt, et al., 2013, p. 5).

However, developing a new drug is a time-consuming and cost-intensive process. It takes an average of twelve years and costs several million euros from inception to approval. The pharmaceutical industry spends a great deal of money developing drugs with improved properties, and new indications and innovations in the supply of medicinal products are both desirable and indispensable. However, they are also a source of conflicts of interest between stakeholders. As shown in figure 1, on the one hand, there is a service catalogue bursting with high-quality and innovative drugs that should be fully available for patients. On the other hand, you have the limited resources of the SHI and the demand for sustainable financing. At the same time, the pharmaceutical industry must be supported and rewarded appropriately for the development of innovation. Thus, a "conflict arises between the industrial policy objective of promoting Germany as a location for innovation and the social policy objective of reducing expenditure" (Kohler, 2013, p. 21).

Figure 1: The conflict on the pharmaceutical supply market

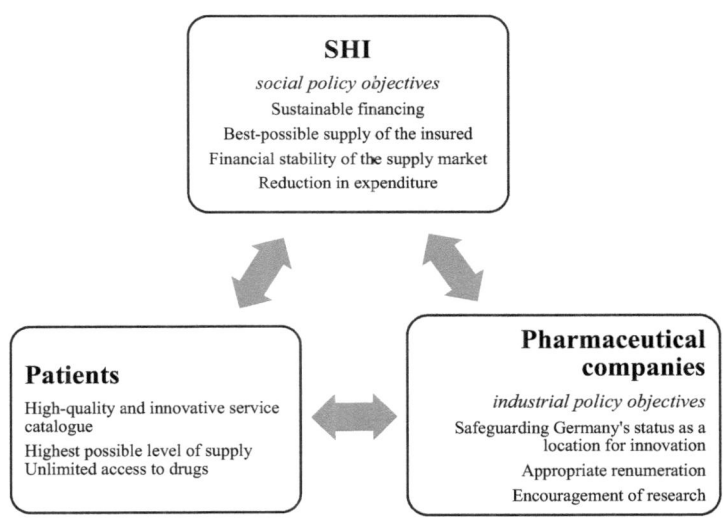

Source: Own diagram

"The medicinal products market is like no other. It's the realm of public health and thus a prerequisite for participation in society" (Wasem, 2012, p. 27). The healthcare decision-makers are therefore increasingly coming under the spotlight when it comes to deciding on optimal diagnostic and therapeutic measures. Thus health policy is also obliged to navigate its way through the medicinal products market and thus also juggle the expenditure on medicinal products with the help of effective instruments. Clinical studies and medical publications are of significant importance and are part and parcel of the on-going trend towards evidence-based medicine (Evans, et al., 2013, p. 20). For example, in recent years, a variety of policy measures has been introduced to keep down the expenditure of the SHIs. "Of the 30 regulatory instruments that existed up until the entry into force of the AMNOG at the beginning of 2011, 24 targeted a limitation of drug expenditure (price or quantity)" (Cassel & Ulrich, 2012, p. 58).

Back in 2007, the SHI Competition Enhancement Act stipulated that the IQWiG could be delegated by the G-BA with a benefit or cost-benefit assessment, primarily designed to find a "reimbursement amount" that appropriately remunerates the added benefit of newly authorised drugs (paragraph 35b of Volume V of the German Social Code). However, "the management tools introduced up until 2011 [...] were unable to bring about the desired balance between heightened efficiency and cost containment in the field of the supply of medicinal products" (Köhler, 2013, p. 21). This can be put down to the fact that, until the entry into force of the AMNOG, pharmaceutical companies were able to set the prices for new drugs themselves, regardless of whether the drugs could produce an added benefit over existing drugs or not. The costs incurred were particularly high and spiralled (Federal Ministry of Health, 2010). The therapeutic added benefits and a fair balance of interests with respect to unreasonably high prices were often questionable. A survey showed that Germany was "a high-price country for non-fixed-price controlled medicinal products, the only country - apart from Malta – with no price regulation for such preparations and the largest European market and reference price country in the international pricing system" (Dingermann, 2013, p. 770). As a consequence, some aspects of the pharmaceutical products market changed with the introduction of AMNOG, as the market - as the name of the Act already implies – was "reformed". According to the Federal Ministry of Health", the Act "paves the way for fair competition and a stronger focus on patient welfare" (Federal Ministry of Health, 2013b). The objectives pursued are presented in the following section.

2.2 The objectives of the Act

The AMNOG sets out to achieve three goals: structural changes, reduction of over-regulation and short-term savings. These measures are intended to cut costs by € 2 billion per year. Above all, however, the legislator is hoping for cheaper innovations for the German market (Federal Ministry of Health, 2013b).

The following objectives of the law have no role to play in the context of this study, but for the sake of completeness are described briefly[3]:

---

[3] More detailed information on this can be found for example on the website of the Federal Ministry of Health.

To counteract over-regulation, under the AMNOG, on the one hand, the two-opinion process (clause 73 d) and, on the other hand, the merit/demerit pricing system have been abolished. (Federal Ministry of Health, 2013b). Increasing the pharmacy rebate from 1.75 to 2.05 euros per pack of a prescription drug is a way of cutting costs for the health insurance funds in the short term. "The wholesale trade will lose a total of about 200 million euros in favour of the funds, of which EUR 170 million for the SHI" (Bergh, 2010, p. 5). Furthermore, the health insurance funds are set to save 300 million euros per year, as vaccine manufacturers in Germany are not allowed to charge higher prices than the major countries of the EU. Another example of cost-containment measures are cytostatic drugs[4]. If these are given as an infusion, in future only "fair market settlement prices" are to be agreed. Savings of 100 million euros annually are expected here by the SHI (Bergh, 2010, p. 5).

The structural changes mainly concern the newly introduced assessment of the added benefit and thus the early benefit assessment. In the context of this survey, the focus will be put on this part in particular, which is examined in detail in section 2.4.

---

[4] Cytotoxic drugs are "drugs used in chemotherapy that inhibit the growth of cancer cells, but that can also damage normal tissue" (GBE, 2013).

2.3 The Federal Joint Committee (G-BA)

Before illustrating the early benefit assessment procedure, it is first necessary to give an outline of the body known as the Federal Joint Committee (G-BA). This is the decision-making body in the field of early benefit assessment.

Figure 2: Distribution of seats and structure of the Federal Joint Committee

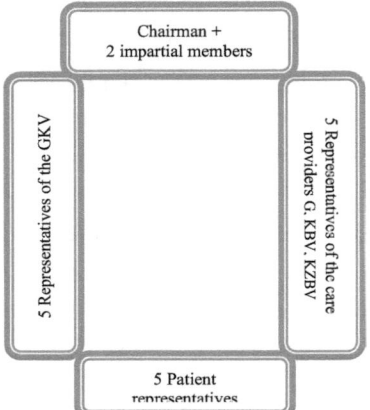

Source: Own diagram

"The Federal Joint Committee (G-BA) is a legal entity under public law and is formed by the four major umbrella organisations of self-management in the German healthcare system (see figure 2): the Confederation of Contract Doctors and Dentists, the German Hospital Federation and the Central Federal Association of Statutory Health Insurance Funds" (G-BA, 2013a). The G-BA also has three impartial members, one of which is the Chairman of the body. Thus, the G-BA is composed of 13 voting members. The meetings of the G-BA can also be attended by five representatives of the patients. These are not entitled to vote, but may submit proposals.

The G-BA is the supreme decision-making body for health-related topics and comes under the legal supervision of the Federal Ministry of Health. The G-BA is divided into nine sub-committees. The medicinal products subcommittee deals with the early benefit assessment. The names of the members of the Committee are subject to strict confidentiality in order to avoid possible interference (G-BA, 2013b).

2.4 The Institute for Quality and Efficiency in Healthcare

The Institute for Quality and Efficiency in Healthcare (IQWiG) was established in 2003 as part of the SHI Modernisation Act. It operates under the auspices of self-management in the German healthcare system. The Institute has received a general mandate from the G-BA, i.e. it can also independently tackle themes and deal with them in so-called "working papers". Its task is to examine the benefits and harms of medical measures. Furthermore, the IQWiG receives concrete assignments from the G-BA. "The Institute draws up professionally independent, evidence-based (substantiated) reports, for example, on:

• medicinal products

• non-pharmacological treatments (e.g., surgical procedures)

• methods of diagnosis and early detection (screening)

• treatment guidelines and disease management programmes (DMP) "(IQWiG, no date).

As such, the Institute does not conduct studies on its own account, but draws on existing studies and scientific publications.

The IQWiG is divided into three services (quality assurance, information management and law) and eight departments (medicinal product assessment, non-pharmacological methods, health economics, quality of care, health information, medical biometry, communication and administration) (IQWiG, 2013a, p. 47 -51).

IQWiG is financed by charges for inpatient and outpatient medical care under the statutory health insurance system. These charges are determined each year by the G-BA according to the budget of the IQWiG.

Starting out with eleven staff members, the Institute now has 166 employees (see figure 3). 34 of the new jobs were created as a result of the AMNOG. In 2012, 37 employees were working in the field of medicinal product assessment (IQWiG, 2013A, pp. 47-51).

Figure 3: Scope of the work of the IQWiG

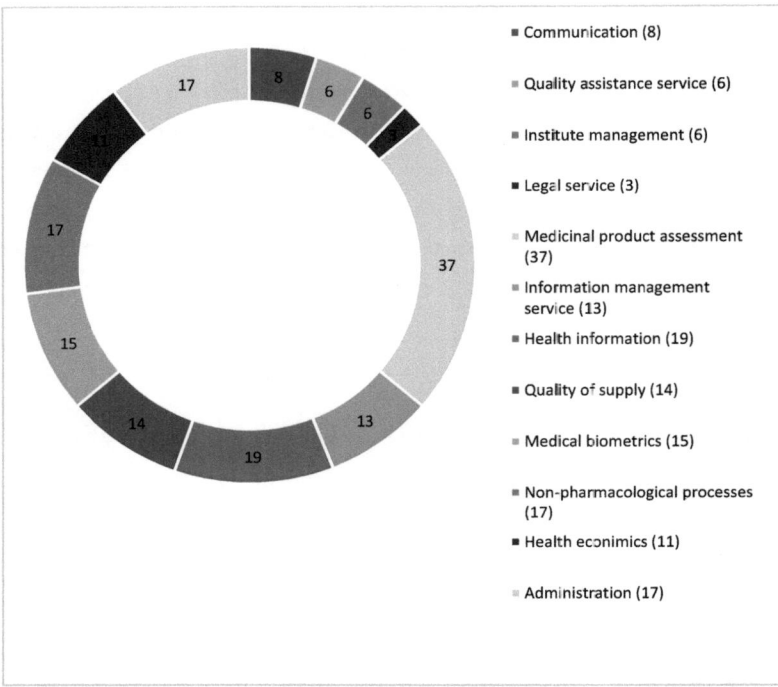

Source: own diagramm according to IQWiG, 2013a, p. 44

Under the AMNOG, the IQWiG is assigned two new tasks: on the one hand, it assesses the dossier of the pharmaceutical manufacturer and draws up a benefit assessment on this basis. On the other hand it draws up a cost-benefit assessment in the event of an unsuccessful arbitration award (the complete early benefit assessment procedure is discussed in detail in section 2.6). This survey shall focus solely on the benefit assessment however, since the drawing up of a cost-benefit assessment in the context of AMNOG has not been necessary so far (IQWiG, 2013a, p. 18).

2.5 The manufacturer dossier

In order to demonstrate that the new drug is also an innovation, the pharmaceutical company in question is invited to submit a standardised dossier to the G-BA. The structure and content of this dossier is presented below. Figure 4 illustrates the scope and relations of the different modules of the dossier.

Figure 4: Structure of the dossier

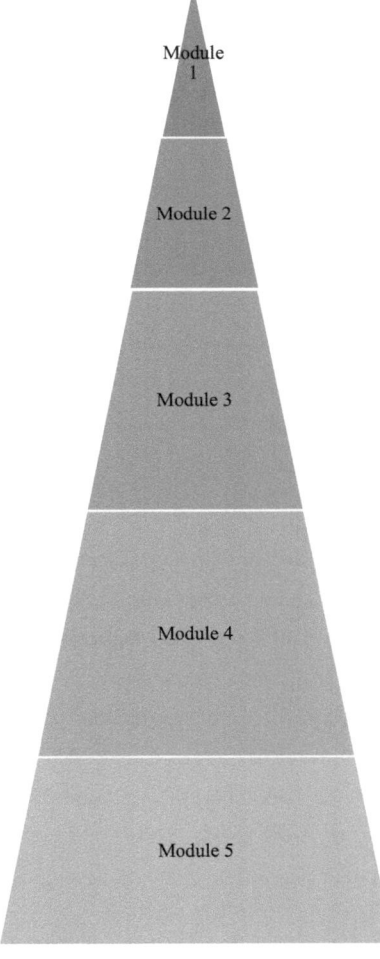

Module 1 contains the administrative information. This is also where the statements of the dossier are summarised.

The second module includes general statements about the medicinal product. Furthermore, the indications are named.

Module 3 contains the appropriate comparator therapy, the number of patients with therapeutically significant added benefits, the cost of the treatment for the SHIs and the requirements for a quality assured application.

Module 4 comprises a systematic overview of medical benefits and medical added benefits, a description of the methodology and the results and details of the patient groups, for which there is a therapeutically significant added benefit.

Module 5 contains the appendices.

This is where the full text of the cited sources, files for the documentation of information gathering, reports of all studies of the pharmaceutical company, essential

Source: Own Source: Own diagram according to IQWiG, 2013b

21

authorisation documents, assessment report of the authorising authority and a checklist for testing the formal completeness can be found (IQWiG, 2013b).

To ensure a consistent format, the G-BA provides the pharmaceutical company with templates that need to be filled out accordingly. The complete dossier must then be submitted electronically as a DVD in duplicate and no later than four weeks after the authorisation of the medicinal product to the G-BA (G-BA, 2013c).

According to paragraph 5 section 1 of the Ordinance on the Benefit Assessment of Pharmaceuticals (AM- NutzenV): "The added benefit must be proven by the pharmaceutical company in the dossier according to paragraph 4. The Federal Joint Committee has no obligation to examine the facts of its own motion."

2.6 Early benefit assessment

One of the measures introduced by the AMNOG is the benefit assessment of medicinal products. This means that newly authorised medicinal products are subject to an early benefit assessment. That being said, "the Federal Joint Committee can order a benefit assessment even for medicinal products already authorised before the 1st of January 2011 and placed on the market (so-called existing market)" (German Parliament, 2013). On the basis of a benefit assessment, a possible added benefit is to be appraised over an appropriate comparator therapy in order to counteract inappropriate medicinal product prices through fair price negotiations.

All the guidelines for the early benefit assessment are anchored in the Ordinance on the Benefit Assessment of Pharmaceuticals. During the benefit assessment, the medicinal products are assigned to one of the benefit categories laid down by the legislator in this ordinance. These are "significant added benefit", "substantial added benefit", "minor added benefit", "added benefit not proven", "added benefit not quantifiable", or "no assessment due to an incomplete dossier". In the event of 'no assessment due to an incomplete dossier" the result is interpreted as "no added benefit". In addition, the reliability of the assertion can be expressed by the very strong "proof", the weaker "evidence" and finally by "indication". It is further possible to grant an "exemption" from the assessment, giving the reasons.

In this book, the focus is on early benefit assessment and the procedure involved is presented in chronological order. Paragraph 2 of the Ordinance on the Benefit

Assessment of Pharmaceuticals sets out definitions for medicinal products with new active ingredients, the benefits of medicinal benefits and added benefits of a medicinal product. These definitions also apply to this survey:

"(1) medicinal products with new active ingredients within the meaning of this Ordinance are medicinal products containing active ingredients, whose effects are not widely known the first time they are authorised by medical science. A medicinal product with a new active ingredient within the meaning of this Ordinance shall be deemed as a medicinal product with a new active ingredient as long as document protection exists for a medicinal product approved for the first time.

[...]

(3) The benefits of a medicinal product within the meaning of this Ordinance is the patient-relevant therapeutic effect in particular with regard to the improvement of health, the shortening of the duration of the disease, the prolongation of survival, reduction of side effects or a better quality of life.

(4) The added benefit of a medicinal product within the meaning of this Ordinance is a benefit within the meaning of paragraph 3, which is quantitatively or qualitatively greater than the benefit of the appropriate comparator therapy."

The current early benefit assessment procedure will be explained below and presented graphically in Appendix 1 by way of illustration.

(1) After approval by the European Medicines Agency (EMA) and thus upon the market launch of a new medicinal product, the manufacturer specifies a price, as was the case to date. No later than four weeks after authorisation, the pharmaceutical company must submit a dossier (see section 2.5) to the G-BA. In a previous consultation between the manufacturer and G-BA any outstanding questions are clarified. The comparator therapy is also established in advance by the G-BA.

(2) The G-BA then delegates the IQWiG with the creation of a benefit assessment - an HTA report (Health Technology Assessment). An HTA is based on the basic principle of evidence-based medicine and assesses technologies in the healthcare system. The core of an HTA report is a review of existing studies and medical

publications on the effectiveness and efficiency of the individual technologies to be evaluated (Schöffski & Graf v.d. Schulenburg, 2008, pp. 447-448).

(3) Three months after the submission of the dossier the BGA publishes the IQWiG report publicly on the internet.

(4) This is followed by a hearing at which manufacturers and experts can comment on the results, and put any questions to the G-BA. Comments are also accepted in writing. At such time, associations or patient organisations can also express their opinion on the assessment of the medicinal product. Furthermore, new relevant data may be submitted by the drug manufacturer.

(5) Three months after the publication of the IQWiG report, the G-BA publishes its decision. This is made both on the basis of the IQWiG report and the comments received. Like the IQWiG, the G-BA estimates the added benefit using the benefit categories laid down by the legislator.

To reach the decision, the IQWiG assessment serves only as a recommendation for the G-BA, which can reach a totally different decision (see section 3.1.3). The decision of the G-BA is likewise published on the Internet.

(6) If the medicinal product is not assigned any added benefit, it is classified in the corresponding reference price group[5]. This reference price then represents the maximum reimbursement amount for the SHI.

(7) If it is not possible to classify the medicinal product in a reference price group, negotiations take place between the manufacturers and the Central Federal Association of Statutory Health Insurance Funds (SHI national association). Here agreement is reached on the reimbursed amount, which does not lead to higher annual treatment costs than the appropriate comparator therapy.

---

[5] Comparable medicinal products may be classified into groups, where a maximum amount is allocated for the reimbursement (reference price groups):
Reference price groups Level 1: medicinal products with the same active ingredients,
Reference price groups Level 2: medicinal products whose active ingredients are comparable in pharmacological terms, in particular chemically, and at the same time in terms of their therapeutic effect,
Reference price groups Level 3: medicinal products that are comparable in terms of their therapeutic effect (Federal Ministry of Health, 2013c)

(8) If it is confirmed that the medicinal product has an added benefit, negotiations are held between the manufacturer and the Central Federal Association of Statutory Health insurance funds. If an agreement is reached, a rebate on the manufacturer price is set twelve months following the market launch.

(9) If the Manufacturer and the Central Federal Association of Statutory Health Insurance Funds cannot agree on a rebate, an arbitration board is brought in. Thus an arbitration award is carried out by a neutral officer that mediates between the manufacturer and the Central Federal Association of Statutory Health Insurance Funds. The rebate adopted here shall be set no later than 15 months after the market launch of the product and shall apply retroactively to the original price negotiations twelve months following the market launch. However, up until 30.05.2013, arbitration was necessary in only four cases (Central Federal Association of Statutory Health Insurance Funds, 2013a).

(10)   In rare cases, the rebate will not be accepted. In this case, the IQWiG is once again entrusted with a cost-benefit assessment. The rebate set already by the arbitration board is then valid up to the end of the new procedure. However, this case is yet to occur at the time of writing.

2.7 The special case of orphan drugs

So-called orphan drugs are medicinal products used to treat rare diseases. "A disease is considered rare if not more than 5 in 10,000 people have the specific disease. Around 30,000 diseases are known worldwide, of which more than 5,000 are considered as rare diseases, also called "orphan diseases" (ACHSE 2013). In Germany, about four million people live with a rare disease.

Since often only a few people are affected by the same rare disease, researching and developing new drugs is often not financially profitable and therefore not very lucrative for the pharmaceutical industry. If manufacturers make a turnover of no more than EUR 50 million per year with a preparation for a rare disease, they can apply for an orphan drug status from the EMA. This grants various market and competitive advantages. On the one hand, they benefit from comprehensive scientific support during the development and, on the other, after the market approval, they will be granted a ten-year market exclusivity. During this time, drugs with the same indication cannot be placed on the market (EMA, 2013).

In accordance with paragraph 35a, section 1, sentence 10 of Volume 5 of the German Social Code, the added benefit of orphan drugs is considered as already proven. "Evidence of the clinical benefit and of the medical added benefits in relation to the appropriate comparator therapy does not need to be supplied. [...] The law thus considers that an added benefit is in principle a given for an approved orphan drug without requiring it to be substantiated by an appropriate scientific assessment of the medicinal product" (G-BA, 2013e). So far, the added benefit had not been categorised, so that manufacturers and the Central Federal Association of the Statutory Health Insurance Funds could enter directly into price negotiations. Since March 2012, the G-BA will now decide on the extent of the added benefit of orphan drugs without a prior benefit assessment from the IQWiG. This means that the extent of the added benefit now also has implications for the rebate to be negotiated.

3. Evaluation, findings and experience – Critical analysis

The second part of this survey will begin with an analysis of the results of the medicinal products assessed to date. It will examine the classifications of the added benefit categories before presenting the stakeholders, i.e. the health insurance funds, the pharmaceutical industry and patients and describing the impact of the AMNOG on the stakeholders.

3.1 Evaluation of the added benefit classifications

Between the entry into force of the AMNOG on the 1st of January 2011 and up until the 30.11.2013 a total of 67 early benefit assessments of medicinal products were performed. A complete overview of all assessments can be found in Appendix 2. The most important findings of the evaluation shall be presented in this section.

3.1.1 Methodology

Within the framework of this study, all of the early benefit assessment procedures in accordance with paragraph 35a of Volume 5 of the German Social Code; which were completed up to and including 30.11.2013, were evaluated in the light of the extent of the added benefit. This includes both the dossiers submitted by the pharmaceutical companies, the assessment of the dossier by the IQWiG and the final decisions of the G-BA.

In doing so, the extent of the added benefit is divided into six categories (see section 2.6.)

• "significant added benefit"

• "substantial added benefit"

• "minor added benefit"

• "added benefits not proven"

• "added benefit not quantifiable", or

• "no assessment due to an incomplete dossier".

Furthermore, exemptions and orphan drugs play a separate role. This evaluation will focus primarily on the most reliable results. For this reason, exemptions, orphan drugs and in some cases medicinal products with "non-quantifiable added benefits" shall not be taken into consideration, but are summarised in figures 6 and 7 under "other". Until 30.11.2013, 15 medicinal products came under this category. Nor will the "Proof", "Evidence" and "Indication" levels of confidence be considered in the evaluation.

Furthermore, an individual added benefit shall be determined for each area of application listed by the manufacturer. For example, a drug with three applications can also have three different added benefit classifications. In each case, the highest classification of the added benefit was considered for the evaluation of the data.

3.1.2 Frequency distribution of the added benefit categories

In the early benefit assessment procedure, the added benefit over the appropriate comparator therapy is classified by the various stakeholders on the basis of three points (see table 1):

1) In the dossier of the manufacturer of the medicinal product, it is the first to categorise the added benefit of its own medicinal product. According to data available up until 30.11.2013, the manufacturers claimed the added benefit of their medicinal products over the appropriate comparator therapy 24 times as "significant", 14 times as "substantial" five times as "minor" and three times as "non-quantifiable". Two manufacturers could already see no added benefit in their own dossier and six times no dossier was submitted.

This means that 64.2% of the pharmaceutical companies promised an added benefit of the new medicinal product, while only 3% described no added benefit.

2) Further along the procedure, the IQWiG assesses the submitted dossier and once again assigns an added benefit category. It twice awarded the "significant" category, nine times the "substantial", five times "minor" and twice the category of "non-quantifiable" added benefit. However, it assigned 24 medicinal products to the "no added benefit" category and assessed a total of twelve dossiers as incomplete or missing.
According to the IQWiG, thus only 23.9% of the new medicinal products have an added benefit. Whereas it could confirm no added benefit in 53.7% of cases.

28

3) Ultimately, the G-BA then goes on to assess the added benefits. To date it has not assigned any "significant added benefit". It classified the medicinal products ten times in a "substantial", 16 times in a "minor", twice in a "non-quantifiable" and 19 times in an "unproven" added benefit category.

It therefore assigned an added benefit to 38.8% of the medicinal products and could not detect any added benefit in 38.9%.

However, no standardised method for determining the extent of the added benefit exists to date (Busse, et al., 2013, p. 407).

Table 1: Assigned added benefit categories

	Manufacturer		IQWiG		G-BA	
	Number	*in %*	*Number*	*in %*	*Number*	*in %*
Significant	24	35.8	2	3	0	0
Substantial	14	20.9	9	13.4	10	14.9
Minor	5	7.5	5	7,5	16	23.9
Non quantifiable	3	4.5	2	3	2	3
Unproven	2	3	24	35.8	19	28.4
no/incomplete dossier	6	9	12	17.9	7	10.5
Other	13	19.4	13	19.4	13	19.4

Source: Own diagram

3.1.3 Comparison of the added benefit classifications

The analysis of the different classifications performed in the course of a procedure delivers some interesting results. On the one hand, the nature and extent of the differences between the results of the IQWiG in comparison to those of the G-BA shall be represented below and, on the other, the differences between the evaluation of the pharmaceutical companies and the final results of the G-BA are shown.

3.1.3.1 Differences between the IQWiG and the G-BA

In 58% of cases there was an overlap of the added benefit classification between the decision of the IQWiG and that of the G-BA. In 22% of cases, the G-BA reached a different conclusion: it classified 13% of the medicinal products in a better added benefit category than the IQWiG. In 9% of the dossiers, the extent of added benefit was considered lower (see figure 5).

Figure 5: IQWiG – G-BA decisions

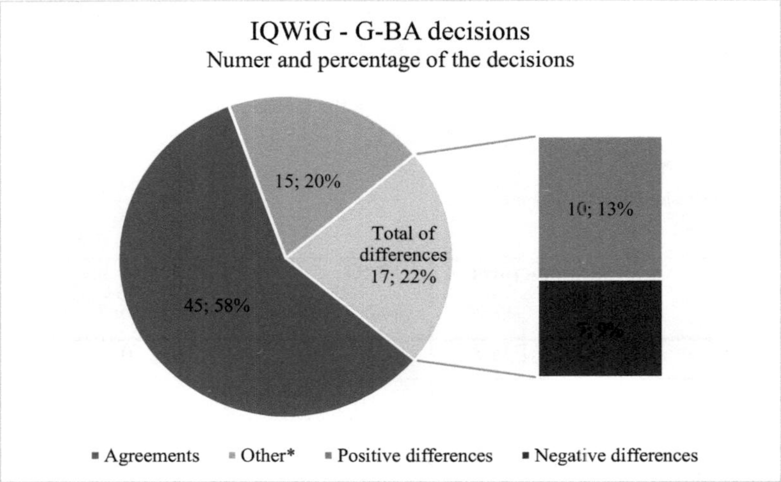

Source: Own diagram, * Exceptions/orphan drugs/non-quantifiable

3.1.3.2 Differences between the pharmaceutical companies and the G-BA

When comparing the classification of the added benefit reached by the pharmaceutical company with the classification of the G-BA decision, the immense impact of the early benefit assessment is clearly visible (see Figure 6):

In only two cases did the added benefit category coincide. This was the assessment of "no added benefit". These are also so far the only two cases in which the pharmaceutical company classified its medicinal product as such. Thus, the G-BA has awarded a dissenting added benefit category in all cases in which the pharmaceutical company has assumed an added benefit. It should also be emphasised that in not one case has it awarded a more positive added benefit than the one awarded by the pharmaceutical company in its dossier.

Figure 6: Pharmaceutical company - G-BA decisions

Pharmaceutical company - G-BA decisions
Number and percentages of the decisions

0; 0%

15; 22%

Total of
differences
50; 75%

50; 75%

2; 3%

■ Agreements   ■ Other*   ■ Positive differences   ■ Negative differences

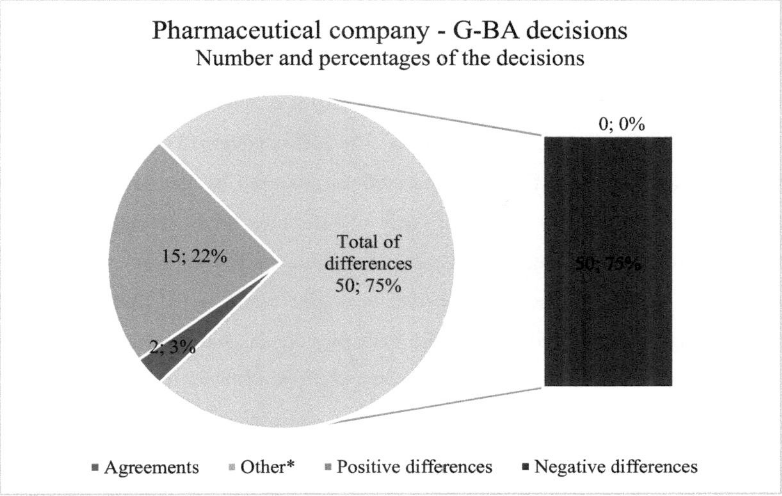

*Source: Own diagram; * Exceptions/orphan drugs/non-quantifiable*

3.2 The impact on the statutory health insurance funds

Since the 1st of January 2009, in accordance with paragraph 193, section 3 of the German Insurance Contract Act (VVG):

> "Every person resident in Germany is obliged to take out a medical expenses insurance with an insurance company licensed to do business in Germany for themselves and for their legal dependents, [...], which includes at least one reimbursement for outpatient and inpatient treatment [...]".

This means that Germany has a general compulsory insurance system. The insured can choose between statutory and private health insurance. Since the statutory insurance funds are represented by the Central Federal Association of Statutory Health Insurance Funds in the G-BA and are thus also involved in the early benefit assessment, they are considered in the following. However, decisions in the context of early benefit assessment apply equally to the private health insurance companies.

3.2.1 Overview of the statutory health insurance funds in Germany

"All funds are public bodies. They are not profit-driven and are based on the principles of self-government" (Busse, et al., 2013, p. 45). In Germany, about 85% of the population are insured by the SHI (Busse, et al., 2013, p. 110). Thus, the SHI is the central pillar of the German healthcare system. The SHI is governed by the principle of solidarity, which means that the costs incurred are covered by the solidarity of the members and their employers. Different types of insurance funds belong to the SHI. They are, according to the Federal Ministry of Health, local health insurance funds, company health insurance funds, guild health insurance funds, social health insurance funds, agriculture, forestry and horticulture insurance funds, and the German pension insurance for miners, railway workers and seamen (Federal Ministry of Health, 2013d).

According to the information available as at July 2013, the BARMER GEK is the biggest health insurance fund with 6.7 million members, followed by the Techniker Krankenkasse with 6.1 million members, DAK-Gesundheit with 4.96 million members, and the AOK Bavaria with 3.28 million members (German Research Foundation, DFG, 2013).

3.2.2 Challenges facing the health insurance funds

The health insurance funds in Germany perform a permanent balancing act (see figure 8). Despite the legally required self-government, the health insurance funds are confronted in many ways with the legal framework conditions.

As such, the funds are exposed to an ever-increasing competitive pressure, as the insured are free to choose their health insurance fund (Busse, et al., 2013, pp. 116-117). As a result, the number of statutory health insurance funds has decreased dramatically over the last 20 years. While there were 1,147 statutory health insurance funds in 1990, there are only 134 in 2013 (see figure 7).

Figure 7: Evolution in the number of statutory health insurance funds

Evolution in the number of statutory health insurance
funds in Germany between 1990 and 2013

Year	Number
1990	1.147
1995	960
2000	420
2005	267
2008	221
2009	202
2010	169
2011	156
2012	146
2013	134

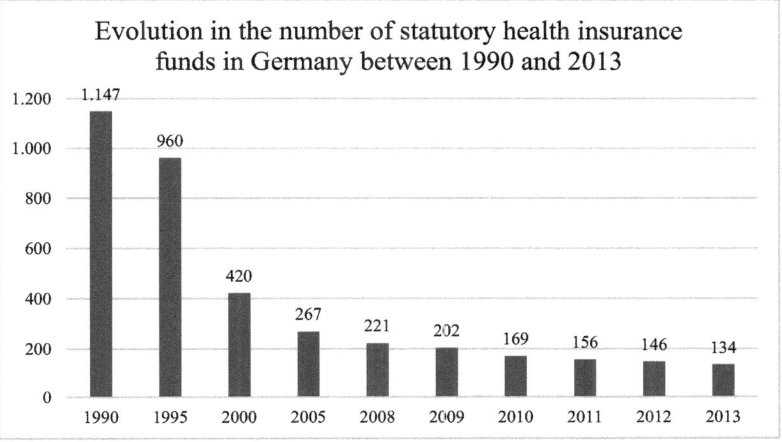

Source: Own diagram according to the Central Federal Association of Statutory Health Insurance Funds, 2013b

In this competitive environment, responsibility over provision plays a major role. The funds are required to offer an innovative range of products and good medical provision while keeping their prices competitive.

The demands of the insured are steadily increasing, because they see it as their duty to find out as much as possible and demand as an informed patient a high quality of healthcare, including drug treatment.

Figure 8: The balancing act of the health insurance funds

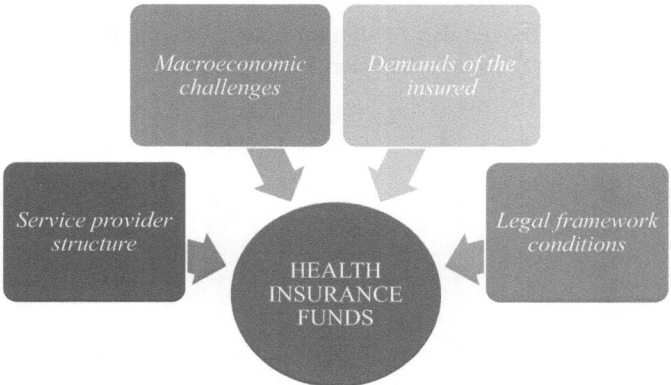

Source: Own diagram

A constantly changing service provider structure that is moving in the direction of the out-patient sector is part of the balancing act. Furthermore, macroeconomic challenges such as high unemployment, low basic wages and demographic change also play an important role for the health insurance funds (Parow, et al., 2011, pp. 71-72).

3.2.3 The Central Federal Association of Statutory Health Insurance Funds

The Central Federal Association of the SHI represents in Germany the interests of the statutory health and long term care insurance funds. By its own testimony it thus represents at the same time the interests of all the statutory insured (Central Federal Association of the Statutory Health Insurance Funds, 2012).

The Central Federal Association of the Statutory Health Insurance Funds consists of the General Assembly, the Board and the Executive Board.

The AOK, the social health insurance funds (Ersatzkassen), BKK, IKK, mining and agricultural insurance funds each appoint two members to the General Assembly. These elect the board.

The Board consists of 31 insurance members and 21 employers' representatives. It takes all decisions, "which are of fundamental importance for the Central Federal Association of Statutory Health Insurance Funds and the health insurance funds" (Central Federal Association of Statutory Health Insurance Funds, 2012).

To assist the Board in its decisions, there is an Advisory Board and four specialised committees on the topics "Fundamental issues and health policy", "Organisation and Finance", "Contracts and supply" and "Prevention, rehabilitation and care".

The Board of the Central Federal Association of Statutory Health Insurance Funds consists of three full-time employees. "The Executive Board manages the Central Federal Association of Statutory Health Insurance Funds and represents it in and out of court, unless otherwise stipulated by the law or other authoritative law for the Central Federal Association of Statutory Health Insurance Funds" (Central Federal Association of Statutory Health Insurance Funds, 2012).

The Central Federal Association of Statutory Health Insurance Funds concludes framework agreements and remuneration agreements for inpatient, outpatient and dental care. It supports the health insurance funds and their state associations in the performance of their duties. In addition, it represents the SHI interests within the framework of self-administration with the service funds at federal level (e.g. Federal Joint Committee) and with regard to the Federal Ministry for Health. It also sets reference prices for medicinal products and devices and maximum amounts for medicinal products.

3.2.4 The early benefit assessment from the perspective of the Central Federal Association of Statutory Health Insurance Funds

3.2.4.1 Selection of the appropriate comparator therapy

In order to determine an added benefit for a new drug, it must be compared with a therapy that is considered as the standard[6] in the field of application. This can be both a drug and a non-drug treatment. If this appropriate comparator therapy is a drug, it must not belong to the same class of active ingredients. The detailed criteria for selecting the appropriate comparator therapy can be found in paragraph 6 of chapter 5 of the Rules of Procedure of the G-BA (G-BA, 2013c).

The appropriate comparator therapy is determined before the start of the procedure, however only after the drug has been approved by the EMA. As a member of the G-BA, the Central Federal Association of Statutory Health Insurance Funds is also involved in the determination. The determination of the comparator therapy is of great importance, since the pharmaceutical company is obliged to provide evidence of added benefit over the appropriate comparator therapy. Furthermore, the rebate for the medicinal product is negotiated based on the price of the comparator therapy (G-BA, 2013f).

The determination of the appropriate comparator therapy is criticised by various parties and will be considered in more detail in section 3.3.1 from the perspective of the pharmaceutical companies.

3.2.4.2 Price negotiations with the pharmaceutical companies

The price negotiations take place according to the principle of "centralised before decentralised". The negotiations are thus held centrally at the federal level, i.e. here the negotiating mandate is entrusted to the Central Federal Association of Statutory Health Insurance Funds. It negotiates a rebate amount with the pharmaceutical companies that then applies to all health insurance funds, both statutory and private. The starting point of the negotiation is the cost of the appropriate comparator therapy. In the negotiation, agreement is reached on a surcharge on these costs (Central Federal Association of Statutory Health Insurance Funds, 2013c).

---

[6] According to the general and recognised data available to medical science

The fact that the Central Federal Association of Statutory Health Insurance Funds is the sole representative of the statutory health insurance funds in the negotiations does not necessarily reflect the competition between funds. It means that the Central Federal Association of Statutory Health Insurance Funds is put here in a special position of power. The individual funds may be more in tune with the interests and needs of their insured. Thus, the Central Federal Association of Statutory Health Insurance Funds can of course decide only according to the "lowest common denominator". However, the "centralised" solution is designed to ensure that all insured can have new and innovative drugs reimbursed at the same time and that the procedure is not delayed by individual negotiations (Jaeckel, 2011, p. 55-56).

3.2.4.3 Savings through the early benefit assessment

The Innovation Report 2013, a scientific study on the supply of innovative medicinal products states:

> "The experience of countries such as Australia, Canada and Great Britain, where a benefit or cost-benefit assessment has long existed, suggests that the goal of reducing expenditure by no means dominates. [...] The ultimate goal of a benefit or a cost-benefit assessment, as provided under AMNOG, is without a doubt to make it possible to introduce cost-effective and high-quality pharmacotherapy and to exclude medicinal products with dubious benefit or analogue preparations from the SHI supply" (Windt et al., 2013, p. 11).

The health insurance funds claim that the emphasis is not put on saving millions of euros, but on the benefit for the patient. Nevertheless, the appropriate comparator therapy, for example is not chosen only based on purely medical criteria, but also based on economic criteria. Furthermore, in its dossier, the manufacturer must, as explained in section 2.5, specify the cost of the medicinal product for the SHI, although it is a pure benefit assessment and not a cost-benefit assessment.

The Central Federal Association of the Statutory Health Insurance Funds criticises the fact that it is not possible without obstacles to completely exclude medicinal products where no added benefit could be confirmed from reimbursement or their prescription. Furthermore, the Central Federal Association of Statutory Health Insurance Funds would prefer to have a cost-benefit assessment at the beginning of the market launch rather than a pure benefit assessment (Central Federal Association of Statutory Health Insurance Funds, 2013d).

Pharmaceutical expenditure decreased in 2011 compared to the previous year by 4%. Drug expenditure for 2014 amounted to EUR 29.4 billion, up by 1.5% over the previous year. They were thus relatively stable (Häussler, et al., 2013, p. 1). For 2012 and 2013, the Central Federal Association of Statutory Health Insurance Funds expects savings totalling around 120 million euros through the negotiated reimbursement amounts (Central Federal Association of Statutory Health Insurance Funds, 2013a).

3.3 The impact on the pharmaceutical industry

The AMNOG heralded a new era for the pharmaceutical industry in Germany: never before was the power of the pharmaceutical companies subject to such restrictions. Until then, they could set the price for their medicinal product as they saw fit - whether appropriate or not. It was then left to the discretion of the health insurance funds or doctors within the framework of treatment freedom whether a possible added benefit could be observed or not. Today, however there is a burden of proof: it is now up to the pharmaceutical companies to demonstrate an added benefit. The SHI thus wants to save millions at the expense of the pharmaceutical industry. "Many pharmaceutical companies fear an abuse of the early benefit assessment" (Dingermann, 2013, p. 770).

3.3.1 The pharmaceutical industry in Germany

In 2012, the pharmaceutical industry in Germany employed about 110,000 people, or almost 7% more than in 2010. "In 2012, the pharmaceutical industry in Germany generated almost 42 billion euro in turnover - 5.5 per cent more than the previous year" (vfa, 2013a, p. 6).

Figure 9: Share of the different sizes of German pharmaceutical companies according to number of employees

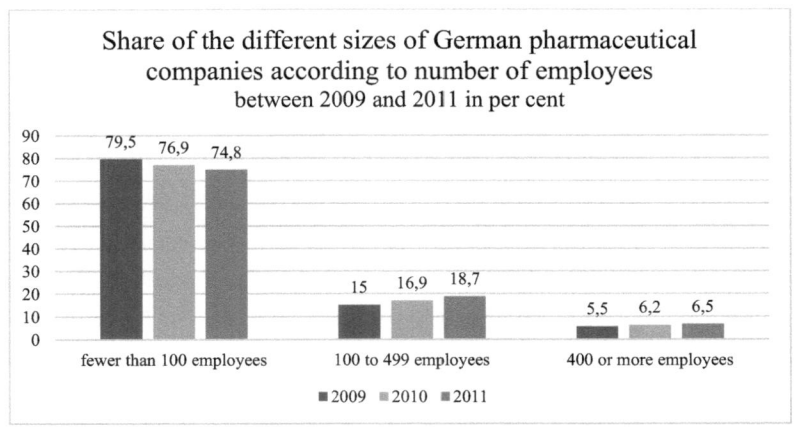

Source: Own diagram according to the BPI, 2013, p. 6

The German pharmaceutical market is mainly made up of small and medium-sized companies (see figure 9). For example in 2011, 74.8% employed fewer than 100 employees and 18.7% between 100 and 499 employees. A mere 6.5% of the pharmaceutical companies had 400 and more employees (BPI, 2013, p. 6).

3.3.2 A critical assessment from the perspective of the pharmaceutical industry

3.3.2.1 Appropriate comparator therapy

"According to the experts, the lynchpin of the early benefit assessment is the determination of the appropriate comparator therapy" (Dingermann, 2013, p. 770). For only after the market approval does the G-BA decide with which existing treatment the manufacturer is to compare its medicinal products. In order to be able to put forward studies that confirm an added benefit over the comparator therapy, the drug manufacturer must however be aware of the comparator therapy before starting the study. This means that chances are that the G-BA will determine an appropriate comparator therapy for which the manufacturer cannot provide studies (BPI, 2010). Indirect comparisons are not accepted as evidence of an added benefit (vfa, 2013b).

Furthermore, there is criticism that Europe-wide therapy standards are considered in the context of the approval by the EMA and studies drawn up on the basis of such standards. The problem is that therapy standards in Europe are not always identical to those in Germany. In its opinion on the AMNOG, the German Pharmaceutical Industry Association therefore demands that the comparator therapies of the G-BA are identical with those granted Europe-wide approval by the EMA (BPI, 2010).

However, a sub-goal in the area of appropriate comparator therapy has already been achieved: In the event that multiple comparator therapies are equally appropriate from medical or evidence viewpoints, then the most economical is automatically selected. In paragraph 6, section 1 of the Ordinance on the Benefit Assessment of Pharmaceuticals of 31 December 2010: "If there are several alternatives, the more economical treatment is to be selected, preferably a treatment for which a fixed amount applies". The rebate to be negotiated on a new drug is based in each case on the price of the comparator therapy. Thus, it could be argued that the rebate has been influenced by a favourable comparator therapy from the beginning (BPI, 2010). But a cheap comparator therapy could also imply that no progress has been made for a long time and that generics are already brought in for comparison. In the event of a positive assessment of the new drug, while there would be a proven case of improved treatment the price awarded would, however, be at a low level.

On the 7th of June 2013, the German Parliament ruled with the "Third Act amending drug and other regulations" that in the future the pharmaceutical company itself would be able to select the appropriate comparator therapy when several treatments have been selected by the G-BA. Thus, paragraph 6, section 2a of the Ordinance on the Benefit Assessment of Pharmaceuticals now states: "If several alternatives are equally appropriate for the comparator therapy according to sections 1 and 2, the added benefit can be demonstrated over any of these therapies". This means that more flexibility was created to ensure that "the available evidence is not lost on formal grounds" (Federal Ministry of Health, 2013e). However, there is still no selection on the basis of purely medical criteria.

3.3.2.2 Cost of the early benefit assessment

The early benefit assessment incurs additional costs for pharmaceutical companies. "Based on 45 companies concerned, for 100 dossiers a year, an additional cost of 125,000 euros can be expected" (German Parliament, 2010). The pharmaceutical companies, however, claimed that each procedure costs them 450,000 to 600,000 euros (vfa, 2013). These costs include translation work for example, since the G-BA requires all studies of the active ingredient to be in German. Twelve months is usually spent compiling the dossier, due to the stringent requirements of the G-BA, an expense that small companies cannot always afford.

Medium-sized companies do not usually have the financial means necessary to cover the costs of research and to develop new drugs but often work on the further development of existing active ingredients. However, this does not allow them to apply for an added benefit, and they are automatically classified in a reference price group. Thus, they cannot negotiate a higher price and at the same time have no incentive to do research on already developed active ingredients (BPI, 2010).

According to the "Pharmaceutical-Atlas 2012", the actual remuneration of the pharmaceutical industry in 2011 fell by 3.3% (iGES, 2012, p. 29).

3.3.2.3 Reference prices under threat

As part of the early benefit assessment, the pharmaceutical companies are obliged to specify their own price and also the drug price in other European countries. This is because the legislator has determined that "the price of the medicinal product in other European countries is to be considered in the negotiation of a rebate amount pursuant to paragraph 130b of volume 5 of the German Social Code" (Central Federal Association of Statutory Health Insurance Funds, 2013e). Thus, the price negotiations are hinged around 15 European countries: Belgium, Denmark, Finland, France, Greece, Great Britain, Ireland, Italy, Netherlands, Austria, Portugal, Sweden, Slovakia, Spain and the Czech Republic. This creates transparency on the one hand, and, on the other, it serves to reduce the prices of innovations at the expense of pharmaceutical companies.

In the pharmaceutical industry, Germany is considered as a "reference price country." So far 19 other European countries base the prices of their medicinal products on the prices in force in Germany (Schwabe & Paffarth, 2012). If the European prices now serve as the basis for negotiations between the Central Federal Association of Statutory Health Insurance Funds and the pharmaceutical companies, this results in a reciprocal price referencing. This can mean huge losses for the drug manufacturers.

It should be noted that, on the one hand, the prices of medicinal products in each country are determined by complex and different factors and that different economic situations prevail in each country. This means that prices of medicinal products in the economically strong Germany were far higher to date than in economically weaker countries such as Greece, Romania, and Spain.

"Given the current international price differences, high price countries have already tried several times to also reduce their prices for medicinal products, preferably with drug imports from low-price countries (parallel and reimports) on the one hand and by referring to low-cost countries in the international price referencing on the other hand" (Cassel & Ulrich, 2012).

Figure 10 shows the price of a patented original preparation against an autoimmune disease in different European countries. For the medicinal product, Germany serves as the reference price (Kanavos, et al., 2011).

Figure 10: Price referencing in Europe

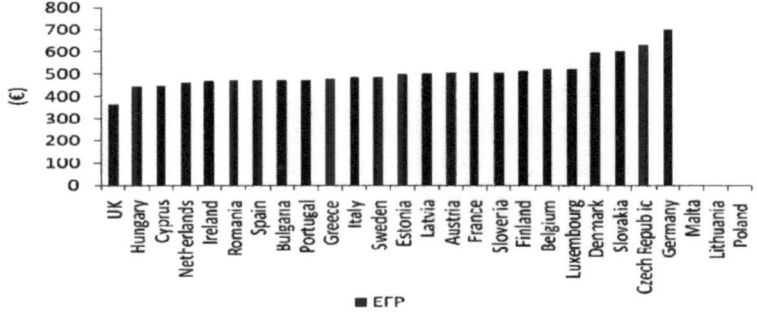

Source: Kanavos, et al., 2011

3.3.2.4 Central Federal Association of the Statutory Health Insurance Funds: rule maker, referee and player

Another aspect that has been criticised by the pharmaceutical industry is the so-called "governance" problem (Häussler, et al., 2013, p. 390). The backdrop to this problem is the power position of the Central Federal Association of the Statutory Health Insurance Funds. Given that it is involved in all stages of the early benefit assessment: it co-determines by its vote in the G-BA the comparator therapy, it is involved in the benefit assessment of the G-BA and it is also a negotiating partner in the price negotiations. Furthermore, representing 90% of the insured, it is even the main buyer of the medicinal products and thus monopolises the demand. A separation of assessment, decision-making and negotiation is indistinguishable. This implies a blatant conflict of interests, making the negotiation of "fair" prices very much questionable (vfa, 2013). The Association of Research-Based Pharmaceutical Companies (vfa) thus dubs the Central Federal Association of Statutory Health Insurance Funds as "Rule maker, referee and player at the same time!" (vfa, 2013).

3.3.2.5 "Opt-out" solution as a consequence

Pharmaceutical companies may be offered a low price as a result of a negative added benefit decision. This can lead to the manufacturer deciding for the "opt-out" solution: In this scenario, which represents the most serious case conceivable, especially for the patients, the manufacturer decides to take the new medicinal product completely off the German market or discontinue its introduction to Germany. Until 31.12.2012, four manufacturers decided to opt out their medicinal products (Häussler, et al., 2013, p. 399).

Manufacturers once again went for this option in 2013. It is particularly alarming that these also included an orphan drug (Bosulif ®) for the treatment of leukaemia patients. According to the manufacturer Pfizer it was not possible "to hold negotiations based on current clinical practice guidelines recommendations for CML treatment and taking into account the orphan drug status of Bosulif" (Pfizer, 2013).

The Central Federal Association of the Statutory Health Insurance Funds, however, considers it "exaggerated [...] to present this retreat of the pharmaceutical companies as a threat that Germany could be cut off from a modern drug supply" (Central Federal Association of the Statutory Health Insurance Funds, 2013f).

3.3.2.6 Flood of data versus employees

Another point that is criticised by the pharmaceutical companies is the sheer scope of the dossier and the associated reliability of the evaluation, which is conducted within a tight deadline (vfa, 2013). As explained in section 2.4, the IQWiG employs 37 people for the assessment of medicinal products. These are responsible for the evaluation of the dossiers submitted. A dossier usually includes several thousand pages (Baertschi & Runge, 2013). On the 1st of April 2013 for example eight dossiers were submitted at the same time, all of which had to be assessed within three months.

3.4 The impact on patients

As we have seen, according to the legislator and the SHI, patients have most to gain from the AMNOG. "The protest of the expert panels makes it [...] clear that the concerns of 'stronger consideration for patient welfare' as one of the primary objectives of the AMNOG will probably fall short of the mark" (Dingelman, 2013, p. 774). However, the patient simply lacks a voice and the power to actively and effectively enforce their concerns. In the wake of AMNOG, more and more patient organisations and self-help groups are now actively lobbying for the reimbursement of the required treatments and drugs.

3.4.1 Patient organisation in Germany

The group of patients is very heterogeneous due to the sheer spectrum of diseases. Sufferers of the same disease usually come together within patient organisations and self-help groups, of which there are many. However, there is no umbrella organisation representing the interests of patients in Germany and, given that it is impossible to elect patient representatives, this makes the inclusion of patients often difficult. Nevertheless, since 2004 there is the possibility of patient involvement in the G-BA:

> "Organisations that significantly represent at the federal level the interests of patients and the self-help of chronically ill and of disabled people in Germany have a consultation right and right to convene meetings within the G-BA in accordance with the requirements of Volume Five of the German Social Code (SGB V) but no voting right" (G-BA, 2013g).

According to the "Regulation on the involvement of patients in statutory health insurance", organisations whose internal order complies with democratic principles and which are neutral and independent, can be recognised. This was confirmed for the German Disability Council, the Federal Association of Patient Interest Groups, the German Association of Self-help Groups e.V. and the Consumer Federation e.V. They should cover a wide range and thus ensure the participation of a variety of stakeholders.

3.4.2 A critical analysis from the patient's perspective

3.4.2.1 Patient involvement in the early benefit assessment

By participating in the G-BA, selected patient representatives are involved in both the determination of the appropriate comparator therapy as well as in the decision on the added benefit. However, here they have merely a right of consultation, i.e. only an indirect influence is possible as, while their votes may be recorded, they are not counted.

The Institute has developed a special questionnaire to ensure that when assessing the dossier "early on important information about the disease and its treatment are obtained from the patient's perspective" (IQWiG, 2013a, p. 29). However, as described in section 3.3.2.6, the limited period of three months as well as the sheer amount of data and documents cannot be overlooked. The IQWiG stated that these special questionnaires were included in only 50% of the assessments. However, the transparency of the answers also comes in for criticism (Stoschek, 2013). Following publication of the IQWiG assessment, patient organisations can submit an opinion and thus express their concerns. In the subsequent hearing, two representatives can then express their views again per opinion (G-BA, 2013h).

Patients participate to a large extent in the financing of the G-BA and the IQWiG. This is secured ultimately by the patients themselves through extra charges for inpatient and outpatient medical treatments (G-BA, 2011).

3.4.2.2 Inadequate "patient-relevant outcomes"

The added benefit of a medicinal product is determined in the early benefit assessment on the basis of "patient-relevant outcomes". These are mortality, symptoms and complaints (morbidity), side effects and health-related quality of life. At the end of 2012, IQWiG conducted a study into the outcomes in the light of 21 completed dossier assessments. "All the investigated dossiers contained patient-relevant outcomes, especially information on morbidity and side effects. Statements about mortality and quality of life, on the other hand, were few and far between" (IQWiG, 2013A, p. 10). Furthermore, in this study, the IQWiG classified 80% of the outcomes specified in the dossiers as relevant to patients. Statements about quality of life and mortality are extremely important. This is particularly true for those affected by serious illness or diseases in the final stage, such as in oncology, where drugs are usually very expensive.

However, data on mortality and quality of life can here impact positively on the benefit side (Glaeske, 2012).

But often the problem lies also in the studies. At the time of the early benefit assessment, no data is usually available on the prolonged use of the medication. Thus, no statements can be made on negative or positive long-term effects. Furthermore, at this time the suitability for daily use cannot be appreciated (Ruof, et al., 2013).

Finally, we can also ask the question of whether the value and benefits of innovation should not be individual. For example, the same medical measure may benefit one patient but could however harm another patient with different characteristics. Age or the will to live, for example, often play a role with patients. Thus, the benefit of a medicinal product is also impacted by the patient himself (Hansen & Lee, 2011, p. 123). These individual criteria are not taken into account during a benefit assessment.

3.4.2.3 Innovations in practice

Despite the selection of "actual" innovations by the early benefit assessment, according to the latest findings, these often do not reach the patient. "The aim of AMNOG was to allow patients direct access to innovative medicinal products. The present data suggest that this objective may have only partially been achieved to date" (Busse, et al., 2013, p. 405). The fact that the manufacturer must demonstrate the added benefit separately for certain fields of application and patient groups means that the G-BA restricts the possible added benefit to a small proportion of patients. Furthermore, it is assumed "that alternatives - including both established and newer active ingredients – enter into competition with the active ingredients to be assessed" (Häussler, et al, 2013, p. 407). Thus "tried and tested" innovations also need a few years until they penetrate the market. Another point is that the AMNOG may have regulated the prices of medicinal products but, on the other hand, recourses in drug prescription have not been abolished. Therefore, doctors are still encouraged to consider their choice of treatment not only on purely medical grounds, but also on economic grounds. Thus, according to the "Ärztezeitung", the Central Federal Association of the Statutory Health Insurance Funds urged doctors to prescribe new drugs "with extreme caution until the final benefit assessment" (Winnat, 2013).

3.4.2.4 Patients turning into experts

Many patients express concern that their treatment or a medicinal product will no longer be reimbursed to them by the health insurance fund in future. That is why those affected are becoming experts themselves and preparing themselves for the worst case scenario.

A practical example is intended to represent the commitment of the parties concerned: haemophilia is an X-linked genetic disease. Due to the genetic deficiency of a clotting factor, blood clotting in outer and inner bleeding is delayed. If the bleeding disorder is not treated, it often leads to life-threatening bleeding or serious damage to the musculoskeletal system. A lifelong substitution therapy is therefore essential (World Federation of Haemophilia (WFH), 2012). In Germany, the number of haemophiliacs requiring permanent treatment is estimated at between 4,000 and 6,000 (German Haemophilia Society (DHG), 2006). The treatment is very expensive however. For example, one unit of a substitution drug costs about 0.70 euros. Depending on the severity of the disease and the therapy approach, a sufferer requires between 100,000-200,000 units per year, in some cases even more (CSG, 2007).

Haemophiliacs are therefore concerned that statutory health insurance will no longer be able to reimburse new medicinal products or treatments (prophylaxis) implying a high consumption of drugs in future. This concern prompted the European Haemophilia Consortium to organise a workshop on "Economics and HTA" in London between the 13th and 15th of September 2013, where 20 patient representatives from 15 European countries had the opportunity to learn in two days about medical benefit assessment and their impact on the treatment of haemophilia. The workshop offered lectures on the economic opportunities of medical benefit assessment and the advantages and disadvantages of HTAs. To put forward their arguments in a reimbursement debate, it is also important for patients to know how the different results come about and what influences them. Patients should get involved from the beginning of the benefit assessment process and be duly informed.

Furthermore, patient representatives from Sweden, France and England shared their experiences in the workshop. In these countries, a benefit assessment of haemophilia treatment has already taken place or is in the works. This means that patient organisations can learn from each other also at international level with an emphasis on networking. At the end of the workshop the theory is applied to various scenarios including a simulated conversation with a Minister of Health.

3.5 Conclusion

The evaluation of the appreciations and decisions on the added benefits of new medicinal products showed significant divergences. The pharmaceutical companies were extremely positive about the added benefits of their medicinal products. However, the G-BA did not endorse the positive assessment one single time. This could be an indication that the pharmaceutical companies actually overestimate the added benefits of their drugs. This is supported by the significant overlaps of the appreciations of the IQWiG and G-BA. The positive differences of the G-BA over the IQWiG showed that patient organisations and associations may still have a possibility of influencing the final assessment in the hearing procedure.

The funds emerge as the "winners". The Central Federal Association of the Statutory Health Insurance Funds celebrates the AMNOG as a "huge success" (Osterloh, 2013). The only criticism it voices is that drugs without added benefits cannot be taken completely off the market. However, the Central Federal Association of the Statutory Health Insurance Funds has a co-determination right in all stages of the decision and benefits from the millions of euros of savings made. We can only hope here that the new position of power is not ultimately exploited at the expense of patients, but that these savings are passed on to the insured, to ensure stable and low insurance premiums. A separation of powers and thus a separation of the stages should be thoroughly considered.

The pharmaceutical companies are the "losers" in the benefit assessment of medicinal products. In the event of a comparator therapy that differs from the EMA, it is sometimes not possible for them to submit the required studies. Furthermore, due to the determination of the appropriate comparator therapy, the rebate to be negotiated at the end is established from the beginning, undermining all hopes of a "fair" price negotiation. The company is deprived of any pricing power. Thus there is no incentive for smaller development advances, although these are often important. There are also additional costs and the workload for the preparation of the dossier. These charges primarily affect small and medium-sized companies.

Since Germany is considered as a reference price country on the pharmaceutical market, prices from 15 other European countries are also taken into account in the price negotiation between the manufacturer and Central Federal Association of Statutory

Health Insurance Funds, resulting in a reciprocal price referencing. The consequence could be that medicinal products are no longer first put on the market in Germany but in other European countries, which are used in the future as the price reference country. In the most serious case, however, the pharmaceutical companies could decide for the "opt-out" solution, depriving patients in Germany of that particular drug. From a critical point of view, the concern could be that the production of medicinal products is shifted in future to low-wage countries and that thus the quality of the medicinal products could suffer.

Weighing up the interests of patients the following became clear: according to the legislator, they should be the ones to benefit the most, but it transpires that while they finance the bulk of the implementation of the early benefit assessment via their insurance contributions, they have no voting rights. During a benefit assessment of a new drug, the added benefit for patients is to be evaluated. In addition, the patients are also those who are affected by an illness and who are partly lifetime dependent on an appropriate treatment. It is only logical, therefore, that they should also have a right to be actively involved in the decisions. Unfortunately, the patient lacks an overarching body that can represent their concerns in an effective manner.

Furthermore, "an assessment can only appreciate the status quo at the time it is conducted [...] . Beyond this, future aspects have a prognostic character. For this spectrum, an increased level of outcome uncertainty must be accepted" (Heinemann et al., 2011, p. 152). That is why the decisions of the early benefit assessment should not be final. Thus, even long-term effects could be taken into account and a better and secure assessment made about the patient benefits.

With the AMNOG, the patients are entrusted with a completely new role with new responsibilities. They must now become experts themselves and set themselves up as a network in order to influence the future reimbursement of their treatments.

4 Summary and Outlook

With the Act on the Reform of the Market for Medicinal Products, which entered into force on the 1st of January 2011, the balance of power of the pharmaceutical market changed fundamentally. Therefore, the survey set out to answer this research question:

What impact does the early benefit assessment in the context of the Act on the Reform of the Market for Medicinal Products (AMNOG) have on the stakeholders of the healthcare system?

To answer this question, the theoretical foundations were first laid down in relation to the law, the early benefit assessment and the bodies involved. Subsequently, the previous assessments were evaluated and the view of the selected stakeholders presented. The question could be answered as follows:

The Central Federal Association of the Statutory Health Insurance Funds as the representative of the statutory health insurance funds has gained in power: it is now involved as a member of the G-BA in the assessment of the added benefits of a drug and decides on this basis also on the future of the price to be reimbursed. The pharmaceutical companies, however, are losing their clout, and must bow to the specifications and assessments of the G-BA. Consequences such as the "opt-out" solution should be monitored and taken seriously. Patients have both advantages and disadvantages through the AMNOG. They are the ones that are ultimately dependent on the medicinal product and its improvement. However, they have no right to vote in the early benefit assessment procedure.

Finally, it should be noted that economic decisions must be taken due to the limited resources of the healthcare system, so that healthcare remains affordable in the future. Therefore, it is completely justified and even necessary to assess costly drugs with little benefit for the patient. Since the costs are borne by the community of solidarity, even patients themselves should be aware about their costs and weigh up the personal benefits of a new drug for themselves. Prices and prescriptions of medicinal products must be economically viable and cost-efficient, but it must be made clear in the context of the early benefit assessment that efficiency and cost rebate are not equivalent. A modification of the early benefit assessment should certainly be considered.

In future, evaluations in the healthcare system will play an increasingly important role, putting centre stage issues such as rationalisation and prioritisation, which have remained taboo in Germany to date. In countries such as England or Sweden, it is already happening. There, decisions are clearly taken on the basis of cost-benefit analyses of up to what price a drug is refundable. Furthermore, a decision is made on the basis of criteria such as age, disease and self-influencing risk factors, for which patients a drug is reimbursed. In the light of demographic change and the associated rising healthcare costs, it is probably inevitable that this topic will soon reach the discussion tables in Germany.

Now it remains to be seen how the German government of the 18th legislative period will approach its public health responsibility, especially to come closer to the goal of "stronger consideration for patient welfare" within the framework of the AMNOG (Federal Ministry of Health, 2013e).

Bibliography

Baertschi, G. & Runge, C., 2013. Erfahrungen mit der frühen Nutzenbewertung aus Sicht der Industrie. In: Strategien für mehr Effizienz und Effektivität im Gesundheitswesen. Berlin: PL Academic Research, pp. 169-181.

Bergh, W. v. d., 2010. Innovationen unter Druck. Ärzte Zeitung, December, p. 5.

Federal Ministry of Health, 2010. Die Spreu vom Weizen trennen - Das Arzneimittelmarktneuordnungsgesetz, Berlin: Federal Ministry of Health.

BPI, 2010. Stellungnahme des Bundesverbandes der Pharmazeutischen Industrie, Berlin: German Pharmaceutical Industry Association.

BPI, 2013. Pharma-Daten 2013, s.l.: German Pharmaceutical Industry Association, p. 6.

Busse, R., Blümel, M. & Ognyanova, D., 2013. Das deutsche Gesundheitssystem. Berlin: Medizinisch Wissenschaftliche Verlagsgesellschaft, p. 45.

Cassel, D. & Ulrich, V., 2012. Herstellerpreise auf eropäischen Arzneimittelmärkten als Erstattungsrahmen in der GKV-Arzneimittelversorgung. Duisburg, Essen, Bayreuth: Universität Duisburg/Essen, Universität Bayreuth, p. 58.

Dingermann, T., 2013. Das Arzneimittelmarktneuordnungsgesetz (AMNOG) und seine Folgen. Der Internist. 54. P. 770

Evans, I., Thornton, H., Chalmers, I. & Glasziou, P., 2013. Wo ist der Beweis?. Bern: Verlag Hans Huber, p. 20.

G-BA, 2013c. Verfahrensordnung, Berlin: Federal Joint Committee.

Glaeske, G., 2012. Das Dilemma zwischen Wirksamkeit nach AMG und patientenorientiertem Nutzen. Deutsches Ärzteblatt, 17 February, Jg. 109(7), pp. 115-116.

Hansen, H. P. & Lee, A, (2011). Patients aspects and involvement in HTA: an academic perspective. Health Technology Assessments and Rare Diseases. Odense, Denmark. p. 124

Heinemann, A.-K. & Lang, C. Der Begriff der frühen Nutzenbewertung nach dem AMNOG. 2011. Medizinrecht. 29(3). p. 152

Häussler, B., Höer, A. & Hempel, E., 2013. Arzneimittel-Atlas 2013. Berlin: Springer Medizin. pp. 381-407

iGES, 2012. Arzneimittel-Atlas 2012, Berlin: iGES. p. 29.

IQWiG, 2013a. Jahresbericht 2012, Köln: Institute for Quality and Efficiency in Healthcare, pp. 29-51.

IQWiG, 2013b. Erstellung und Einreichung eines Dossiers zur Nutzenbewertung gemäß § 35a SGB V, Institute for Quality and Efficiency in Healthcare.

IQWiG, 2013c. Kosten und Nutzen in der Medizin, Berlin: Institute for Quality and Efficiency in Healthcare.

Jaeckel, R., 2011. Stellenwert selektiver Vertrags- und Versorgungsformen nach dem AMNOG: eine arzneimittelpolitische Betrachtung und Bewertung. In: Innovatives Versorgungsmanagement. Berlin: MWV Medizinisch Wissenschaftliche Verlagsgesellschaft, pp. 55-56.

Kanavos, P., Schurer, W. & Vogler, S., 2011. The Pharmaceutlical Distribution Chain in the European Union: Structure and Impact on Pharmaceutica Prices. London Wien: EMINeT, pp. 58-60

Köhler, A., 2013. In: Das gebrochene Preismonopol der Pharmaindustrie. Baden-Bade: Nomos Verlagsgesellschaft, p. 21.

Osterloh, Falk, 2013. Arzneimittelmarktneuordnungsgesetz: Der Zusatznutzen ist belegt. Deutsches Ärzteblatt; 110(26): A-1296 / B-1136 / C-1124.

Parow, D., Czerner, T. & Erbe, C., 2011. AMNOG - Neue Vertragsmöglichkeiten mit pharmazeutischen Unternehmen aus Sicht der DAK. In: Innovatives Versorgungsmanagement. Berlin: MWV Medizinisch Wissenschaftliche Verlagsgesellschaft, p. 71-72.

Ruolf, J., Schwartz, W., Schulenberg, J.-M. & Dintsios, C.-M , 2013. Early benefit assessment (EBA) in Germany: analysing decisions 18 months after introducing the new AMNOG legislation. Springer.

Schwabe, U. & Paffarth, D., 2012. Arzneimittelverordnungs-Report 2012, Berlin: Spriner Medizin.

vfa, 2013a. Die pharmazeutische Industrie in Deutschland, Köln Berlin: German Association of Research-based Pharmaceutical Companies, p. 6.

vfa, 2013b. Stellungnahme zu den Erfahrungen der forschenden Pharmaunternehmen mit dem Arzneimittelmarktneuordnungsgesetz (AMNOG), Berlin.

Wasem, J., 2012. Der Gesundheitsökonom. Hilfe! Zwischen Krankheit, Versorgung und Geschäft, p. 27.

Schöffski, O. & Graf v.d. Schulenburg, J.-M., 2008. Health Technology Assessment (HTA). In: Gesunheitsökonomische Evaluationen. Berlin: Springer-Verlag, pp. 447-448.

Windt, R., Boeschen, D. & Glaeske, G., 2013. Innovationsreport 2013, Bremen: Techniker Krankenkasse, pp. 5-11.

Winnat, C., 2013. Die KVen spielen mit alten Regressängsten. Ärzte Zeitung, 03 June 2013.

Electronic media

ACHSE, 2013. ACHSE.
Available under: http://achse-online.de/cms/die_achse/warumachse/warumachse.php
(28 November 2013).

Federal Ministry of Health, 2013a. Health insurance - Key figures and rules of thumb.
Available under:
http://www.bmg.bund.de/fileadmin/dateien/Downloads/Statistiken/GKV/Kennzahlen_D
aten/KF2013Bund_Juli_2013.pdf (16 October 2013)

Federal Ministry of Health, 2013b. The Act on the Reform of the Market for Medicinal
Products (AMNOG).
Available under:
http://www.bmg.bund.de/krankenversicherung/arzneimittelversorgung/arzneimittelmark
tneuordnungsgesetz-amnog/das-gesetz-zu-neuordnung-des-arzneimittelmarktes-
amnog.html (15 October 2013)

Federal Ministry of Health, 2013c. Fixed amounts (medicinal products).
Available under:
http://www.bmg.bund.de/krankenversicherung/arzneimittelversorgung/arzneimittelmark
tneuordnungsgesetz-amnog/glossar-zum-amnog.html (23 October 2013)

Federal Ministry of Health, 2013d. Tasks and organisation of the SHI.
Available under:
http://www.bmg.bund.de/krankenversicherung/grundprinzipien/aufgaben-und-
organisation-der-gkv.html (4 December 2013)

Federal Ministry of Health, 2013e. Press release.
Available under
http://www.bmg.bund.de/fileadmin/dateien/Pressemitteilungen/2013/2013_02/130607_
PM_Dritte_AMG_Novelle_BT_2_3_Lesung.pdf (03 December 2013)

German Parliament, 2013. Communication of the Federal Government on the Decision
of the Bundesrat on a Bill on the Reform of the Market for Medicinal Products within
statutory health insurance (AMNOG).
Available under: http://dipbt.German parliament.de/dip21/brd/2013/0598-13.pdf
(3 December 2013)

German parliament, 2010.
Available under: http://dip21.German parliament.de/dip21/btd/17/024/1702413.pdf
(26 October 2013)

CSG, 2007. Haemoassist - Quality assurance in hemophilia treatment with the help of
an electronic documentation system.
Available under:
http://www.iges.de/e1154/e4356/e4394/e5297/e5842/e5843/programitem5862/Schoen_
ger.pdf (8 December 2013)

DFG, 2013. Large statutory health insurance funds in Germany according to number of
members in 2013 (in millions; Version: 1 July 2013).
Available under: http://de.statista.com/statistik/daten/studie/218457/umfrage/groesste-
gesetzliche-krankenkassen-nach-anzahl-der-versicherten/ (4 December 2013)

DHG, 2006. DHG.
Available under: http://www.dhg.de/index.php?id=108 (7 December 2013)

EMA, 2013. Orphan designation.
Available under:
http://www.ema.europa.eu/ema/index.jsp?curl=pages/regulation/general/general_conten
t_000029.jsp&mid=WC0b01ac05800240ce (28 November 2013)

G-BA, 2011. Financing.
Available under: http://www.g-ba.de/institution/aufgabe/finanzierung/ (23 November
2013)

G-BA, 2013a. Members.
Available under: http://www.g-ba.de/institution/struktur/mitglieder/ (13. November
2013)

G-BA, 2013b. Structure, Members, Patien participation.
Available under: http://www.g-ba.de/institution/struktur/ (13 November 2013)

G-BA, 2013e. Question about the special case of orphan drugs.
Available under: http://www.g-
ba.de/institution/themenschwerpunkte/arzneimittel/nutzenbewertung35a/fragen/#abschn
itt-4 (28 November 2013)

G-BA, 2013f. Questions about the appropriate comparator therapy.
Available under: http://www.g-
ba.de/institution/themenschwerpunkte/arzneimittel/nutzenbewertung35a/fragen/#abschn
itt-5 (24 November 2013)

G-BA, 2013g. Patient participation.
Available under: http://www.g-ba.de/institution/struktur/patientenbeteiligung/
(3 December 2013)

G-BA, 2013h. Questions about the hearing procedure.
Available under: http://www.g-
ba.de/institution/themenschwerpunkte/arzneimittel/nutzenbewertung35a/fragen/#abschn
itt-9 (2 December 2013)

G-BA, no date. Since when is there patient participation in the Federal Joint
Committee?.
Available under: http://www.g-ba.de/institution/sys/faq/zur-faq-
kategorie/10/#details/51:52:48 (4 December 2013)

GBE, 2013. Cytostatic drugs.
Available under: http://www.gbe-
bund.de/gbe10/abrechnung.prc_abr_test_logon?p_uid=gasts&p_aid=&p_knoten=FID&
p_sprache=D&p_suchstring=9558::Zytostatika (13. Dezember 2013)

Central Federal Association of Statutory Health Insurance Funds, 2012. Committees.
Available under: http://www.gkv-
spitzenverband.de/gkv_spitzenverband/wir_ueber_uns/gremien/gremien.jsp (17.
November 2013)

Central Federal Association of Statutory Health Insurance Funds, 2013a. Press release - The "AMNOG" Medicinal Product Act is a success.
Available under: http://www.gkv-spitzenverband.de/presse/pressemitteilungen_und_statements/pressemitteilung_52736.js p (15 October 2013)

Central Federal Association of Statutory Health Insurance Funds, 2013b. All statutory health insurance funds.
Available under: http://www.gkv-spitzenverband.de/krankenversicherung/krankenversicherung_grundprinzipien/alle_ges etzlichen_krankenkassen/alle_gesetzlichen_krankenkassen.jsp
(26 November 2013)

Central Federal Association of Statutory Health Insurance Funds, 2013c. Rebate negotiations.
Available under: http://www.gkv-spitzenverband.de/krankenversicherung/arzneimittel/rabatt_verhandlungen_nach_amno g/fragen_und_antworten_amnog/sb_rabatt_verhandlungen_fragen_und_antworten.jsp
(3 December 2013)

Central Federal Association of Statutory Health Insurance Funds, 2013d. Where do the health insurance funds see problems with the AMNOG?.
Available under: http://www.gkv-spitzenverband.de/krankenversicherung/arzneimittel/rabatt_verhandlungen_nach_amno g/fragen_und_antworten_amnog/sb_rabatt_verhandlungen_fragen_und_antworten.jsp
(4 December 2013)

Central Federal Association of Statutory Health Insurance Funds, 2013e. Which European price serves as a starting point?.
Available under: http://www.gkv-spitzenverband.de/krankenversicherung/arzneimittel/rabatt_verhandlungen_nach_amno g/fragen_und_antworten_amnog/sb_rabatt_verhandlungen_fragen_und_antworten.jsp
(5 December 2013)

Central Federal Association of Statutory Health Insurance Funds, 2013f. Why have some pharmaceutical companies stopped selling their drugs in Germany?.
Available under: http://www.gkv-spitzenverband.de/krankenversicherung/arzneimittel/rabatt_verhandlungen_nach_amno g/fragen_und_antworten_amnog/sb_rabatt_verhandlungen_fragen_und_antworten.jsp
(4 December 2013)

IQWiG, not date About us.
Available under: https://www.iqwig.de/de/ueber_uns/aufgaben_und_ziele.2946.html
(30 November 2013)

Pfizer, 2013. Failure of negotiations with the Central Federal Association of Statutory Health Insurance Funds on the drug Bosulif (Bosutinib).
Available under:
http://www.pfizer.de/medien/meldungen/meldung/news/verhandlungen-mit-dem-gkv-spitzenverband-zum-medikament-bosulif-bosutinib-gescheitert.htm (3 December 2013)

Stochek, Jürgen, 09.12.2013. Benefit assessment not yet patient-relevant. Ärzte Zeitung. Available under:
http://www.aerztezeitung.de/politik_gesellschaft/arzneimittelpolitik/nutzenbewertung/article/850807/leitartikel-nutzenbewertung-noch-nicht-patientenorientiert.html (15 December 2013)

WFH, 2012. Hemophilia.
Available under: http://www.wfh.org/en/page.aspx?pid=646 (6 December 2013)

List of figures

List of tables

List of appendixes:

Appendix

Appendix 1: The early benefit assessment procedure

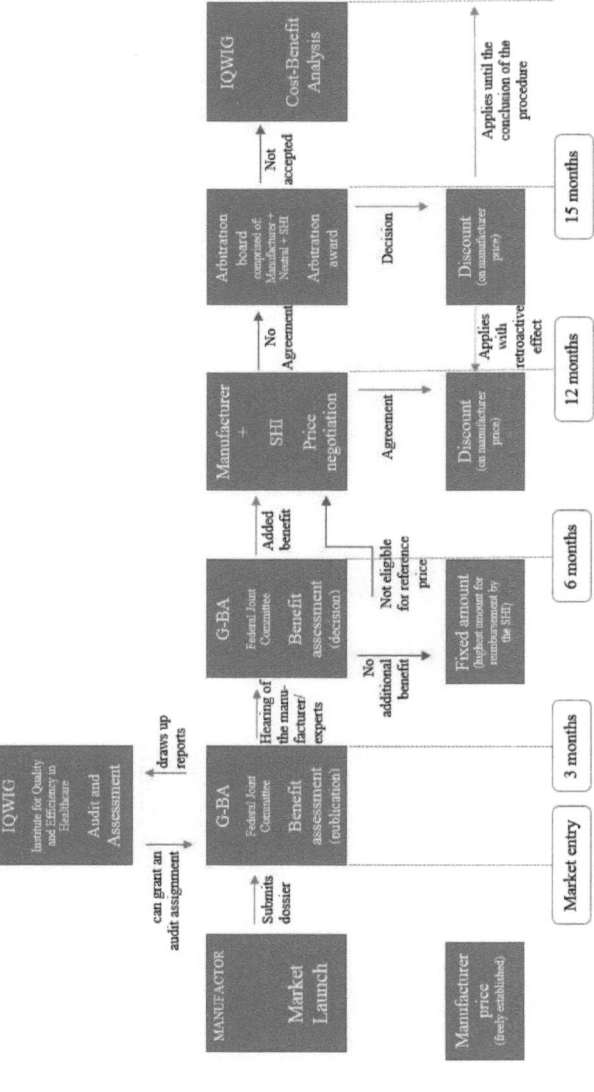

Source: own image according to :

http://www.bmg.bund.de/service/medien.html?tx_bmgmedia_pi1?tx_bmgmedia_pi1[content]=7570&tx_bmgmedia_pi1[controller]=Page&cHash=9a1ca1d89c7cf63993d23064497b161a

Appendix 2: the early benefit assessment decisions

Early benefit assessment decisions in accordance with paragraph 35a of Volume V of the German Social Code

Up until 30.11.2013

Legend:
- significant added benefit
- substantial added benefit
- minor added benefit
- added benefit not proven
- added benefit not quantifiable
- exemption
- no/incomplete dossier

Active ingredient	Trade name	Manufacturer Company	Added benefit	IQWiG Decision	G-BA Decision	G-BA Decision
Ticagrelor	Brilique®	AstraZeneca GmbH	significant added benefit	substantial added benefit	substantial added benefit	15.12.2011
Ceftarolinfosamil	Zinforo®	AstraZeneca GmbH	exemption	exemption	exemption	03.05.2012
Cabazitaxel	Jevtana®	Sanofi-Aventis Deutschland GmbH	significant added benefit	minor added benefit	minor added benefit	29.03.2012
Fingolimod	Gilenya®	Novartis Pharma GmbH	significant added benefit	added benefit not proven	minor added benefit (IFN-β 1a in patients with quickly progressing severe multiple sclerosis)	29.03.2012
Regadenoson	Rapiscan®	Rapidscan Pharma Solutions EU Ltd.	incomplete dossier	incomplete dossier	incomplete dossier	29.03.2012
Eribulin	Halaven®	Eisai GmbH	significant added benefit	added benefit not proven	minor added benefit	19.04.2012
Microbial Collagenase from Clostridium histolyticum	Xiapex®	Pfizer Pharma GmbH	significant added benefit	added benefit not proven	added benefit not proven	19.04.2012

Substance	Product	Manufacturer				Date
Aliskiren/Amlodipine	Rasilamlo®	Novartis Pharma GmbH	substantial added benefit	added benefit not proven	added benefit not proven	03.05.2012
Retigabin	Trobalt®	GlaxoSmithKline GmbH & Co. KG	added benefit not quantifiable	added benefit not proven	added benefit not proven	03.05.2012
Pitavastatin	Livazo®	Merckle Recordati GmbH	no dossier	no dossier	no dossier	18.08.2011
Apixaban	Eliquis®	Bristol-Myers Squibb GmbH & Co. KGaA	substantial added benefit	minor additional benefit on hip joint-OP	minor added benefit	07.06.2012
Cannabis Sativa	Sativex®	Almirall Hermal GmbH	substantial added benefit	added benefit not proven	minor added benefit	21.06.2012
Dexmedetomidine	Dexdor®	Orion Corporation	exception	exception	exception	18.08.2011
Belatacept	Nulojix®	Bristol-Myers Squibb GmbH & Co. KGaA	substantial added benefit	minor added benefit	minor added benefit	05.07.2012
Belimumab	Benlysta®	GlaxoSmithKline GmbH & Co. KG	significant added benefit	added benefit not proven (as different comparator therapy)	significant added benefit	02.08.2012
Fampridin	Fampyra®	Biogen Idec GmbH	significant added benefit	added benefit not proven (as no usable studies available)	added benefit not proven	02.08.2012
Ipilimumab	Yervoy®	Bristol-Myers Squibb GmbH & Co. KGaA	significant added benefit	substantial added benefit	substantial added benefit	02.08.2012
Bromfenac	Yellox®	Bausch & Lomb/ Dr. Mann Pharma	no dossier	no dossier	no dossier	19.01.2012
Boceprevir	Victrelis®	MSD SHARP & DOHME GmbH	significant added benefit	added benefit not quantifiable (in patients without cirrhosis)	indication of an added benefit, extent not quantifiable	01.03.2012
Pirfenidon	Esbriet®	InterMune Deutschland GmbH	orphan drug/substantial added benefit	added benefit not proven	added benefit not quantifiable/ orphan drug	15.03.2012
Abiraterone acetate	Zytiga®	Janssen-Cilag GmbH	significant added benefit	substantial added benefit	substantial added benefit	29.03.2012
Linagliptin	Trajenta®	Boehringer Ingelheim GmbH	no added benefit	added benefit not proven	added benefit not proven	29.03.2012
Telaprevir	Incivo®	Janssen-Cilag GmbH	significant added benefit	added benefit not quantifiable	added benefit not quantifiable	29.03.2012
Tafamidis Meglumin	Vyndaqel®	Pfizer Pharma GmbH	orphan drug/significant added benefit	orphan drug	minor added benefit	07.06.2012
Entricitabine/ Rilpivirine/ Tenofovir Disoproxil	Eviplera®	Gilead Sciences GmbH	significant added benefit	incomplete dossier	minor added benefit	05.07.2012

Rilpivirine	Edurant®	Janssen-Cilag GmbH	minor added benefit	substantial added benefit	minor added benefit	05.07.2012
Azilsartan Medoxomil (as potassium salt)	Edarbi®	Takeda Pharma GmbH	incomplete dossier	incomplete dossier	no dossier submitted	15.03.2012
Ceftarolinfosamil	Zinforo®	AstraZeneca GmbH	exemption	exemption	exemption	03.05.2012
Vemurafenib	Zelboraf®	Roche Pharma AG	significant added benefit	substantial added benefit	substantial added benefit	06.09.2012
Vandetanib	Caprelsa®	AstraZeneca GmbH	significant added benefit	incomplete dossier	incomplete dossier	06.09.2012
Piperaquinte traphosphate, Dihydroartemisinine	Eurartesim®	sigma-tau Arzneimittel GmbH	exemption	exemption	exemption	03.05.2012
Pasireotide	Signifor®	Novartis Pharma GmbH	orphan drug/significant added benefit	orphan Drug	minor added benefit	06.12.2012
Tegafur, Gimeracil, Oteracil	Teysuno®	Nordic Pharma GmbH	no dossier	no dossier	no dossier	20.12.2012
Ivacaftor	Kalydeco	Vertex Pharmaceuticals GmbH	orphan drug/significant added benefit	orphan drug	substantial added benefit in adults (from 12 years), minor added benefit in children	07.02.2013
Linagliptin	Trajenta®	Boehringer Ingelheim International GmbH	added benefit not proven	added benefit not proven	added benefit not proven	21.02.2013
Perampanel	Fycompa®	Eisai GmbH	significant added benefit	added benefit not proven	added benefit not proven	07.03.2013
Ruxolitinib	Jakavi®	Novartis Pharma GmbH	orphan drug/substantial added benefit	orphan drug	minor added benefit	07.03.2013
Aclidinium bromide	Eklira® Genuair® / Bretaris® Genuair®	Almirall Hermal GmbH	minor added benefit	added benefit not proven	added benefit not proven	21.03.2013
Axitinib	Inlyta®	Pfizer Pharma GmbH	substantial added benefit	Sorafenib: substantial added benefit; Everolimus: added benefit not proven	indication: minor added benefit	21.03.2013
Decitabine	Dacogen®	Janssen-Cilag GmbH	substantial added benefit	orphan Drug	minor added benefit	02.05.2013
Crizotinib	Xalkori®	Pfizer Pharma GmbH	significant added benefit	added benefit not proven	**substantial added benefit (Patients with chemotherapy) added benefit not proven (Patients without chemotherapy)**	02.05.2013

Drug	Brand	Company			Date
Saxagliptin/Metformin	Komboglyze®	AstraZeneca GmbH & Bristol-Myers Squibb GmbH CO. KG	minor added benefit	added benefit not proven	minor added benefit (dual combination therapy Saxagliptin/Metformin Added benefit not proven (triple combination therapy Saxagliptin/Metformin + Insulin)	02.05.2013
Brentuximab Vedotin	Adcetris®	Takeda Pharma Vertrieb GmbH & Co. KG	orphan drug	orphan drug	not quantifiable	16.05.2013
Linagliptin	Trajenta®	Boehringer Ingelheim International GmbH	no dossier	no dossier	no dossier	16.05.2013
Pixantrone	Pixuvri®	CTI Life Sciences Ltd	added benefit not quantifiable	added benefit not proven, as relevant data not available	added benefit not proven	16.05.2013
Aflibercept	Eylea®	Bayer Vital GmbH	added benefit not quantifiable	added benefit not proven	added benefit not proven	06.06.2013
Dapagliflozine	Forxiga®	Bristol-Myers Squibb GmbH & Co. KGaA/ AstraZeneca GmbH	substantial added benefit	added benefit not proven	added benefit not proven	06.06.2013
Apixaban	Eliquis®	Bristol-Myers Squibb GmbH & Co. KGaA / Pfizer Deutschland GmbH	significant added benefit	ASS: substantial added benefit; VKA: < 65 added benefit not proven, >65 indication substantial added benefit	minor added benefit	20.06.2013
Fidaxomicine	Dificlir®	Astellas Pharma GmbH	significant added benefit	Added benefit not proven, as corresponding data not available	added benefit not proven (Patients with mild organic histories of Clostridium-difficile-associated diarrhoea) Significant added benefit (patients with severe and/or recurrent histories of Clostridium-difficile-associated diarrhoea)	04.07.2013
Ingenol mebutate	Picato®	LEO Pharma GmbH	substantial added benefit	added benefit not proven	added benefit not proven	04.07.2013
Abirateron acetate	Zytiga®	Janssen-Cilag GmbH	substantial added benefit	substantial added benefit	substantial added benefit	04.07.2013

Substance	Trade name	Company				Date
Aflibercept	Zaltrap®	**Sanofi-Aventis** Deutschland GmbH	significant added benefit	minor added benefit	minor added benefit	15.08.2013
Lixisenatide	Lyxumia®	**Sanofi-Aventis** Deutschland GmbH	minor added benefit	added benefit not proven	added benefit not proven	05.09.2013
Vandetanib	Caprelsa®	**AstraZeneca** GmbH	significant added benefit	added benefit not proven	minor added benefit	05.09.2013
Colestilan	BindRen®	**Mitsubishi** Pharma Deutschland GmbH	significant added benefit	minor added benefit	added benefit not proven	01.10.2013
Pertuzumab	Perjeta®	**Roche** Pharma AG	significant added benefit	significant added benefit	substantial added benefit	01.10.2013
Saxagliptin	Onglyza®	**Bristol-Myers** Squibb GmbH & Co. KGaA / **AstraZeneca** GmbH	Significant added benefit	added benefit not proven	minor added benefit	01.10.2013
Saxagliptin/Metformin	Komboglyze®	**Bristol-Myers** Squibb GmbH & Co. KGaA/ **AstraZeneca** GmbH	minor added benefit	added benefit not proven	added benefit not proven	01.10.2013
Sitagliptin	Januvia®, Xelevia®	**MSD SHARP & DOHME** GmbH	significant added benefit	added benefit not proven, except for: sulfonylurea+metformin: minor added benefit; Glipizide+Metformin: Men - significant added benefit, Women - Indication added benefit	minor added benefit	01.10.2013
Sitagliptin/Metformin	Janumet®, Velmetia®	**MSD SHARP & DOHME** GmbH	significant added benefit	added benefit not proven	minor added benefit	01.10.2013
Vildagliptin	Galvus®, Jalra®, Xiliarx®	**Novartis** Pharma GmbH	substantial added benefit	added benefit not proven	added benefit not proven	01.10.2013
Vildagliptin/Metformin	Eucreas®, Icandra®, Zomarist®	**Novartis** Pharma GmbH	substantial added benefit	added benefit not proven	added benefit not proven	01.10.2013
Linaclotid	Constella®	**Almirall Hermal** GmbH	substantial added benefit	added benefit not proven	Added benefit not proven	17.10.2013
Ocriplasmin	Jetrea®	**ThromboGenics** NV / **Alcon** Pharma GmbH	substantial added benefit	> 60 letters EDTRS: significant added benefit; 35 to 60 letters EDTRS: substantial added benefit	substantial added benefit	17.10.2013
Bosutinib	Bosulif®	**Pfizer** Pharma GmbH	orphan drug/significant added benefit	orphan drug	added benefit not quantifiable	17.10.2013

Retigabine	Trobalt®	**GlaxoSmithKline** GmbH & Co. KG	procedure dismissed	procedure dismissed	procedure dismissed	15.08.2013
Lisdexamfetamine Mesilat	Elvanse®	**Shire** Deutschland GmbH	substantial added benefit	added benefit not proven	added benefit not proven	14.11.2013